THE 4 KEYS TO HEAVEN

MASS
ROSARY
SCAPULAR
WAY OF THE CROSS

"Jesus, Mary, I Love You, Save Souls"

DEDICATION

To Mary we dedicate this booklet of prayers. She has repeatedly said: "Pray! You have to pray!" It is our hope you will find these prayers useful and that you will heed Mary's words: "Pray, dear children. Pray from your heart." We urge you to listen to Her call, to hear Her request. It will be your gateway to eternal salvation.

MARY'S CALL

P.O. Box 162
504 W. U.S. Hwy. 24
Salisbury, MO 65281

Phone: 660-388-5308
Email: maryscall@maryscall.com

www.maryscall.com

MARY'S CALL

Mary's Call is a small, not-for-profit family organization. Our ministry is to encourage prayer, especially the Rosary and Way of the Cross.

The original undertaking of Mary's Call was the production of a 15 decade Rosary tape with meditations plus six hymns. The first order for the tape was received on May 4, 1989 (Ascension Thursday).

We create Mary's Call unique books and have available bibles, rosaries, scapulars, religious books, plaques, and many other items and religious gifts. In order for items to be sold at the lowest price, every effort is made to keep production costs to a minimum and, at the same time, maintain exceptional standards.

Mary's Call remains a very small family organization and is able to operate only through the assistance (time, talent, and donations) of friends. We hope that you will receive many blessings as a result of joining us in this ministry of prayer.

TABLE OF CONTENTS

MY PRAYER

Oh, my God the Father, I offer to Thee this Mass and this Holy Communion which I have just received.

And I unite this offering with all the masses offered, and all the Holy Communions received this day, and every day from the dawn of the Christian era, till the end of time.

I join this with the suffering and death of Jesus Christ, my Lord and Redeemer.

And with all the prayers, works, suffering, zeal and devotion of every member of the mystical body of Christ.

I offer all of this infinite merit to Thee, my heavenly Father, through the most holy name of Jesus, and through Mary Immaculate, my Mother, in reparation for every sin, offense or imperfection that I have ever been guilty of during my entire life.

I also recommend to Thee, each of my dear ones; my relatives, benefactors, friends and enemies; all with whom I come in contact in any way, whether in business, social, or any other relation.

I commend to Thee, in a special way, all who have asked me to pray for them. I recommend to Thee, their petitions, I beg of Thee to grant their requests, if they are in conformity with Thy holy will.

I also beseech Thee to have compassion on our departed, who look to me for prayers; for whom I have been asked to pray, and for whom I have promised to pray. Amen.

BE NOT AFRAID

Live in the faith and hand it on to your children. Love the Church as a mother. Make room in your hearts for all men. Forgive one another and be peacemakers wherever you are.

To those who suffer, I say: "Be confident, for Christ, who has gone before you, will give you strength to face sorrow."

To the youth, I say: "Make a good investment of your life, for it is a precious treasure."

To everyone, I say: "May the grace of God accompany you every day."

— Pope John Paul II

LIFE BEGINS WITH PRAYER

Let us pray and talk to our Heavenly Father.
Family prayer should not be a last resort, it should
be first.
Prayer is life vitamin pills, to build up those who
are run down.

If at first you don't succeed, pray and pray again.
Prayer is a pause that refreshes.

Sometimes prayer is the only solution to the
problems of life. Use the name of Jesus often in
your prayer.

Your joy in life depends much upon your prayers
in life. Prayer is a rain maker that causes showers
of blessings.

He who goes to bed without praying really gets
into a spiritually cold bed.

Prayers are our Stepping Stones to Heaven

11

I SAID A PRAYER FOR YOU TODAY

I said a prayer for you today
And know God must have heard

I felt the answer in my heart
Although He spoke no word!

I didn't ask for wealth of fame
(I knew you wouldn't mind)

I asked Him to send treasures
Of a far more lasting kind!

I asked that He'd be near you
At the start of each new day

To grant you health and blessings
And friends to share your way!

I asked for happiness for you
In all things great and small

But it was for His loving care
I prayed the most of all!

MOTHER TERESA

I want you to realize the tenderness of God's love; I have called you by your name. You are mine. Water of temptation will not drown you. Fire of sin will not burn you. I have carved you in the palm of My hand. You are precious to Me. I love you (from Isaiah 43). Keep the joy of loving God, loving Jesus in your heart, and share that joy with all you meet.

PRAYER OF THANKSGIVING

O my God I thank You for all the benefits which I have ever received from You. Give me light to see what sins I have committed, and grant me grace to be truly sorry for them.

13

MORNING PRAYERS

DAILY OFFERING

O Jesus, through the Immaculate Heart of Mary, I offer you my prayers, works, joys and sufferings of this day, for all the intentions of Your Sacred Heart, in union with the Holy Sacrifice of the Mass throughout the world, in reparation for sin, for the intentions of all my friends and associates, and in particular for the intentions of the Holy Father.

ACT OF FAITH

My God, I believe in You and all that You have taught, because You have said it, and Your word is true.

ACT OF HOPE

I hope in Your promise of eternal life and I ask for Your mercy and strength this day.

ACT OF CHARITY

O my God, I love You with my whole heart and above all things, because You are infinitely good and perfect; and I love my neighbor as myself for love of You. Grant that I may love You more and more in this life, and in the next for all eternity.

14

OTHER PRAYERS

Merciful Jesus, I consecrate myself today and always to Your Most Sacred Heart.

Most Sacred Heat of Jesus I implore, that I may ever love You more and more.

Most Sacred Heart of Jesus, I trust in You!

Most Scared Heat of Jesus, have mercy on us!

Sacred Heart of Jesus, I believe in Your love for me.

Jesus, meek and humble of heart, make my heart like Your heart.

15

PRAYER FOR THE SEVEN GIFTS OF THE HOLY SPIRIT

O Lord Jesus Christ, Who, before ascending into heaven, did promise to send the Holy Spirit to finish Your work in the souls of Your Apostles and Disciples — deign to grant the same Holy Spirit to me, to perfect in my soul the work of Your grace and Your love.

Grant me the Spirit of Wisdom — that I may not be attached to the perishable things of this world, but aspire only after the things that are eternal.

The Spirit of Understanding — to enlighten my mind with the light of Your divine truth.

The Spirit of Counsel — that I may ever choose the surest way of pleasing God and gaining heaven.

The Spirit of Fortitude — that I may bear my cross with You, and that I may overcome with courage all the obstacles that oppose my salvation.

The Spirit of Knowledge — that I may know God and know myself, and grow perfect in the science of the Saints.

The Spirit of Piety — that I may find the service of God sweet and amiable.

The Spirit of Fear — that I may be filled with a loving reverence towards God and may avoid anything that may displease Him.

Mark me, dear Lord, with the sign of Your true disciples, and animate me in all things with Your spirit. Amen.

PRAYER TO ST. JOSEPH

O St. Joseph whose protection is so great, so strong, so prompt before the Throne of God, I place in you all my interests and desires. O St. Joseph do assist me by your powerful intercession and obtain for me from your Divine Son all spiritual blessings through Jesus Christ, Our Lord; so that having engaged here below your Heavenly power I may offer my Thanksgiving and Homage to the most Loving of Fathers. O St. Joseph, I never weary contemplating you and Jesus asleep in your arms. I dare not approach while He reposes near your heart. Press him in my name and kiss His fine Head for me, and ask Him to return the Kiss when I draw my dying breath. St. Joseph, Patron of departing souls, pray for us. Amen.

Say for nine consecutive mornings for anything you may desire. It has seldom been known to fail.

JESUS, HELP ME!

In every need let me come to You with humble trust, saying;
>Jesus, help me!

In all my doubts, perplexities, and temptations;
>Jesus, help me!

In hours of loneliness, weariness and trials;
>Jesus help me!

In the failure of my plans and hopes, in disappointments, troubles and sorrows;
>Jesus help me!

When others fail me, and Your Grace alone can assist me;
>Jesus, help me!

When I throw myself on Your tender Love as Savior;
>Jesus help me!

When my heart is cast down by failure, at seeing no good come from my efforts;
>Jesus, help me!

When I feel impatient, and my Cross irritates me;
>Jesus, help me!

When I am ill, and my head and hands cannot work and I am lonely;
>Jesus, help me!

Always, always, in spite of weakness, falls and shortcomings of every kind;

Most Sacred Heart of Jesus, help me and never forsake me.

A PRAYER OF MANY PRAYERS

Dear Father in Heaven, hear my prayer, and do not turn Your face from those who come to You in their need. Send, now, Your Holy Spirit, to fill my mind, my heart, my soul, with the words and thoughts I want to express. Give Him to me again through Your faithful handmaid, Mary, the Mother of Jesus.

Immaculate Mary, pray with me, and for me, now, and help me to be worthy of Your Son. Bring me now to Jesus. Through the gifts of Your Spouse, the Holy Spirit, help me to express my belief, my trust, my faith and my love for Your Son.

Lord Jesus, I pray in praise, in adoration, in thanksgiving that You are with us. I thank you for my faith, that allows me to know You exist. Help me to be more aware of Your presence. Your gifts,

19

and blessings. Never let me forget that all that I am, all that I have comes from You. It is through Your grace, O Lord. Praise be Your name. Help me to better recognize why You came.

Help me, and all Your people to see that Your presence in the world was our redemption, our salvation. Your death and resurrection was a preview of ours. You showed us victory over death, over the world, victory over Satan. Your resurrection promised us eternal life, if we are willing to take up our Cross and follow You.

Lord Jesus, You are the way, the Lamb of God, the Prince of Peace, the Good Shepherd, the Divine Healer. You brought us the sacraments, the new Church, a new covenant. Lord help us to recognize it is all Yours; that our only right is the right choice … You, or the world.

Lord Jesus, help us to see that mankind cannot solve its own problems, just our own conscience alone, is not enough to guide us. It cannot eliminate all the sin in our life. Our own capabilities cannot eliminate all the sin, the suffering, the pain or the violence in the world, without You. Help us to recognize the meaning of Your words:

WITHOUT ME, YOU CAN DO NOTHING.

It is all around us. Why can't we see?

Lord Jesus, help me to help Your people; Your Church, Your priests and bishops. Your brothers and sisters of all races and creeds. Help me to help them through the one means available to me … prayer!

20

Lord Jesus, give us all a stronger need to pray everyday. Give us an unquenchable thirst for prayer. Above all, Lord, may Your Spirit give us a greater gift of humility. Help us all realize we do not have the power to change all the evils in the world. Only You do! Give me and all Your people, the humility to truly understand and follow Your words:

FATHER NOT MY WILL BUT THINE BE DONE.

Lord, give us the realization that submission to Your will, and answers to our needs, come only through prayer.

Lord Jesus, give us the wisdom to search for You every day in prayer, and to seek first Your will.

Amen

ONE LITTLE ROSE

I would rather have one little rose
From the garden of a friend
Than to have the choicest flowers
When my stay on earth must end.

I would rather have one pleasant word
In kindness said to me
Than flattery when my heart is still
And life has ceased to be.

I would rather have a loving smile
From friends I know are true
Than tears shed round my casket
When this world I've bid adieu.

Bring me all your flowers today
Whether pink, or white, or red;
I'd rather have one blossom now
Than a truckload when I'm dead.

DEDICATION

We all must understand that we have to pray. Prayer is not trifle. Prayer is a dialogue with God. We must hear the voice of God in every prayer. It is not possible to live without prayer. Prayer is life.

Prayer means understanding God. Prayer is knowing happiness. Prayer is for learning to cry. Prayer is for learning to blossom. Prayer is a dialogue with God. Pray every day.

God has been forgotten in our age. We need to find Him again.

ALWAYS THERE

God is watching over you
He's always at your side
Trust in Him to comfort you
To be your strength and guide
God is there to help you
To hear your every prayer
Remember you are not alone
God's love is always there.

PRAYER FOR A BEARER OF GOOD NEWS

Father, Lord of all, let me be a bearer of Good News by an example of a holy life and by utilizing some of my talents and time for the extension of Your Kingdom.

Lord Spirit, give me zeal and enthusiasm for spreading the wealth of spirituality in the Church. Let Her Sacraments become my source of strength and grace to fill souls with hope. Send me at least one soul today that I may tell him the news of Your love. Let the Name of Jesus come quickly to my lips as I reach out to touch the hopeless, the poor and the sick. Let mercy spring forth from my heart at any offense so the world will know. You are a forgiving God.

I give You my sufferings today so many souls will find the light. I give You my love that others will find the way. I give You my day that others my see the reflection of Your face. Help me, Lord Jesus, to change the world and build Your Church.

TRUST HIM

Divine Heart of Jesus
In Thee I trust
Trust Him when the dark clouds assail Thee,
Trust Him when Thy strength is small
Trust Him when to simply trust Him,
Seems the hardest thing of all.
Trust Him, He is ever faithful;
Trust Him, for His will is best,
Trust Him, for the heart of Jesus
Is the only place of rest.
Trust Him then through doubts and sunshine;
All Thy cares upon Him cast,
Till the storms of life are over,
And Thy trusting days are past.

"THE ROSARY AND SCAPULAR ARE INSEPARABLE"

Blessed Virgin Mary to Saint Dominic, "One Day through the Rosary and Scapular I will save the World."

Without Saying to Mary that we venerate Her, love Her and trust Her, we tell Her these things every moment of the day, by simply wearing the Scapular.

"WHOSOEVER DIES CLOTHED IN THIS SCAPULAR SHALL NOT SUFFER ETERNAL FIRE"

Mary's promise to St. Simon Stock - July 16, 1251

The Brown Scapular of Our Lady of Mount Carmel should have deep meaning for you. It is a rich present brought down from Heaven by Our Lady herself. "Wear it devoutly and perseveringly," she says to each soul. "It is my garment. To be clothed in it means you are continually thinking of me, and I, in turn, am always thinking of you and helping you to secure eternal life."

A former prior general of the Carmelite Order, the Most Rev. Kilian Lynch, warned against abusing the scapular devotion. "Let us not conclude," he said, "that the scapular is endowed with some kind of supernatural power which will save us no matter what we do or how much we sin… Fidelity to the commandments is required by those seeking the special love and protection of our Lady."

When life seems impossible - Try praying.

27

A MEDITATION

by Cardinal Newman

God has created me to do Him some definite service. He has committed some work to me which He has not committed to another. I have my mission — I may never know it in this life, but I shall be told it in the next.

I am a link in a chain, a bond of connection between persons. He has not created me for naught. I shall do good, I shall do His work. I shall be an angel of peace, a preacher of truth in my own place while not intending it — if I do but keep His Commandments.

Therefore, I will trust Him. Whatever, wherever I am. I can never be thrown away. If I am in sickness, my sickness may serve Him, in perplexity, my perplexity may serve Him; if I am in sorrow, my sorrow may serve Him. He does nothing in vain. He knows what he is about. He may take away my friends. He may throw me among strangers. He may make me feel desolate, make my spirit sink, hide my future from me — still He knows what He is about.

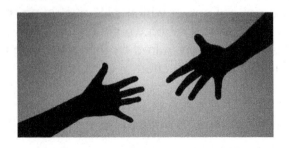

MOST HUMBLE OF US ALL

In trying to know you, Mother
I came to know your Son.
In trying to seek you, Mother,
I only found your Son

In trying to touch you, Mother,
I finally felt your Son.
In trying to hear you, Mother
The words were from your Son.

In trying to make you happy
The joy flowed from your Son.
In trying to love you, Mary,
I have come to love your Son.
Most beautiful of Mothers, you
Are the humble one, for when we try
To reach you, we end up with your Son.

Why can't we find you, Mother,
You must be there with Him. But it's
Jesus that we always find,
In our world growing dim.

Your place above the angels,
Yet humblest of us all.
You always show us Jesus,
No matter how we call.

Most humble of all Mothers,
Your work is finally done.
Thank you blessed Mary,
You have given us your Son.

GOD SHOWS IN YOUR FACE

You don't have to tell how you live each day;
You don't have to say if you work of if you play;

A tried, true barometer serves in the place,
However you live, it will show in your face.

The false, the deceit that you bear in your heart
Will not stay inside where it first got a start;

For sinew and blood are a thin veil of lace -
What you wear in your heart, you wear in your face.

If your life is unselfish, if for others you live,
For not what you get, but how much you can give;

If you live close to God in His infinite grace -
You don't have to tell it, it shows in your face.

*"Lord I shall be very busy this day, I may forget
Thee, but do not Thou forget me."*

PRAYER OF SELF-DEDICATION

Lord Jesus Christ, take all my freedom,
my memory, my understanding, and my will.
All that I have and cherish You have given me.
I surrender it all to be guided by Your will.
Your grace and Your love are wealth enough for
me.
Give me these, Lord Jesus, and I ask for nothing
more.

THE MEMORARE

Remember, O most gracious Virgin Mary, that never was it known that anyone who fled to your protection, implored your help or sought your intercession, was left unaided. Inspired with this confidence, I fly unto you, O Virgin of Virgins, my Mother; to you I come, before you I stand, sinful and sorrowful; O Mother of the Word Incarnate, despise not my petitions, but in your mercy hear and answer me. Amen.

SPIRITUAL COMMUNION

O Jesus I turn toward the holy Tabernacle where You live hidden for love of me. I love you, O my God. I cannot receive you in Holy Communion. Come nevertheless and visit me with Your grace. Come spiritually into my heart. Purify it. Sanctify it. Render it like unto Your own. Amen.

Lord, I am not worthy that thou shouldest enter under my roof, but only say the word and my soul shall be healed.

TREMENDOUS VALUE OF HOLY MASS

At the hour of death the Holy Masses you have heard devoutly will be your greatest consolation.

Every Mass will go with you to Judgment and will plead for pardon for you.

By every Mass you can diminish the temporal punishment due to your sins, more or less, according to your fervor.

By devoutly assisting at Holy Mass you render the greatest homage possible to the Sacred Humanity of Our Lord.

Through the Holy Sacrifice, Our Lord Jesus Christ supplies for many of your negligences and omissions.

He forgives you and all the venial sins which you are determined to avoid. He forgives you all your unknown sins which you never confessed. The power of Satan over you is diminished.

By piously hearing Holy Mass you afford the Souls in Purgatory the greatest possible relief.

One Holy Mass heard during your life will be of more benefit to you than many heard for you after your death.

Through Holy Mass you are preserved from many dangers and misfortunes which would otherwise have befallen you. You shorten your Purgatory by every Mass.

During Holy Mass you knell amid a multitude of holy Angels, who are present at the Adorable Sacrifice with reverential awe.

Through Holy Mass you are blessed in your temporal goods and affairs.

When you hear Holy Mass devoutly, offering it to Almighty God in honor of any particular Saint of Angel, thanking God for the favors bestowed on him, etc., etc., you afford that Saint of Angel a new degree of honor, joy and happiness, and draw his special love and protection on yourself.

Every time you assist at Holy Mass, besides other intentions, you should offer it in honor of the Saint of the day.

PRAYERS WHICH MAY BE SAID AT THE OFFERTORY

When the Priest offers the Host

I place upon the paten my heart; the hearts of all those near and dear to me, especially the hearts of my relatives; the hearts of all those for whom I have promised to pray; the hearts of all those who have injured me; the hearts of all those whom I may have injured; the hearts of all the agonizing.

Jesus, when Thou changes the bread and wine into Thy body and Blood, change our hearts into hearts pleasing to Thee.

When the Priest offers the Chalice

I place within the chalice the souls of all my relatives for whom I should pray; the souls of those for whom I may have forgotten to pray; the souls most devout to the Sacred Heart and the Blessed Virgin; the souls of the most abandoned, Jesus, when Thou changes the wine into Thy Precious Blood, change these poor souls from their place of suffering into Eternal Happiness.

Eternal rest give unto them, O Lord, and let perpetual light shine upon them.

Mother of sorrows! Mother of Christ! You had influence with your Divine Son when on earth, you have the same influence now in Heaven, pray for me, obtain from your Divine Son my request, if it be His Holy Will.

A PRAYER TO THE BLESSED VIRGIN

O most beautiful Flower of Mount Carmel, Fruitful Vine, Splendor of Heaven, blessed Mother of the Son of God, Immaculate Virgin, assist me in this my necessity. O Star of the Sea, help me, and show me herein you are my Mother.

O Holy Mary, Mother of God, Queen of Heaven and Earth, I humbly beseech you from the bottom of my heart, to succor me in the necessity; there are none that can withstand your power.

O, show me herein you are my Mother. O Mary, conceived without sin, pray for us who have recourse to thee. *(3 times)*

Sweet Mother, I place this cause in your hands. *(3 times)*

(With Ecclesiastical Approval)

PRAYER BEFORE A CRUCIFIX

Look down upon me good and gentle Jesus, while before Thy face I humbly kneel and with burning soul pray and beseech Thee to fix deep in my heart lively sentiments of faith, hope and charity, true contrition for my sins and a firm purpose of amendment, while I contemplate with great love and tender pity The Five Wounds, pondering over them within me and calling to mind the words which David Thy prophet said of Thee my Jesus, "They have pierced My Hands and My Feet, they have numbered all My Bones." (Ps. 21, 17-18)

36

KNOWING GOD

I have worked in fertile earth and planted a garden, so I know what faith is.

I have listened to the birds caroling in the early morning and at dusk, so I know what music is.

I have seen the morning without clouds after showers, so I know what beauty is.

I have sat before a wood fire with old friends, so I know what companionship is.

I have walked the paths of quietness along the forest floor, so I know what peace is.

I have dwelt in the valley of remembrance and on the hills of home, so I know what love is.

I have seen the miracle of spring, the fruition of summer, and the beauty of autumn, followed by the response of winter, so I know what life is.

And because, I have perceived all these things, I know what God is.

Turn to God in Prayer

ACT OF PERFECT CONTRITION

O my God, I am heartily sorry and beg pardon for all my sins, not so much because these sins bring suffering of hell to me; but because they have crucified my loving Savior Jesus Christ and offended Your infinite goodness, I firmly resolve, with the help of Your grace to confess my sins, to do penance and to amend my life. Amen.

PRAYER OF THANKSGIVING

I thank You, Jesus for the gift of life, and every moment I live! For my health, even though at times I may have been ill, or suffered serious reverses and sufferings. So often these and other Crosses are blessings in disguise. For the world about me, such as, the glories of nature, the moon, the stars, the flowers of the fields, the fruits of the earth, the very air I breathe, the refreshing rains, the glorious sunshine, the seasons of the year. For my parents, my relatives, my treasured and trusted friends.

I thank You for the gift of my faith. For the gift of Yourself in the Incarnation in which You became man, lived for me, taught me by Your word and example. For the gift of redemption, which You accomplished by Your sufferings, death and resurrection - all this for my salvation.

Oh my God, I thank You for all the favors You have bestowed upon me. I give You thanks from the bottom of my heart for having created me, and for all the joys of life, and its sorrows, too, for the home You gave me, for the loved ones with which You have surrounded me, for the friends I have made through life.

My Lord, I thank You for guarding me always and keeping me safe; for coming to me in Holy Communion, in spite of the coldness of my welcome, for the patient waiting in the adorable sacrament of the altar.

My Jesus, I thank You for having lived, suffered and died for me. I thank You for Your love. I thank You, Lord, for preparing a place for me in Heaven where I hope to be happy with You, and thank You for all eternity. Amen.

THE 4 KEYS TO HEAVEN

MASS
ROSARY
SCAPULAR
WAY OF THE CROSS

"Jesus, Mary, I Love You, Save Souls"

Brother Estanislao (1903 - 1927)

As the age of 18, a young Spaniard entered the Novitiate of Brothers of the Christian School at Bugedo. He took the Vow of Regularity, Perfection and Pure Love. In October, 1926, he offered himself to Jesus through Mary. Soon after this heroic donation, he feel ill, and was obliged to rest. He died saintly in March 1927. He was, according to the Master of Novices, a Privileged Soul, who received messages from Heaven. Confessors and theologians recognized these supernatural facts. His director asked him to write the promises made by our Lord to those who have devotion to the way of the cross.

They are:

1. I'll grant everything that's asked of Me with Faith, when making the Way of the Cross.

2. I promise Eternal Life to those who pray from time to time, The Way of the Cross.

3. I'll follow them everywhere in life and I'll help them, especially at the hour of death.

4. Even if they have more sins than blades of grass in the fields, and grains of sand in the sea, all of them will be erased by The Way of the Cross. (Note: This promise does not eliminate the obligation to confess all mortal sins, and this, before we can receive Holy Communion.)

5. Those who pray The Way of the Cross often, will have a special glory in Heaven.

6. I'll deliver them from Purgatory, indeed if they go there at all, the first Tuesday or Friday after their death.

7. I'll bless them at each Way of the Cross, and My blessing will follow them everywhere on earth and, after their death, in Heaven for all Eternity.

8. At the hour of death I won't permit the devil to tempt them; I'll lift all power from him in order that they'll repose tranquilly in My Arms.

9. If they pray with true love, I'll make each one of them a living Ciborium in which it will please Me to pour My grace.

10. I'll fix My Eyes on those who pray The Way of the Cross often; My hands will always be open to protect them.

11. As I am nailed to the Cross, so also will I always be with those who honor Me in making The Way of the Cross frequently.

12. They'll never be able to separate themselves from me, for I'll give them the grace never again to commit a Mortal sin.

13. At the hour of death I'll console them with My Presence and we'll go together to Heaven. Death will be sweet to all those who have honored Me during their lives by praying The Way of the Cross.

14. My Soul will be a protective shield for them, and will always help them, whenever they have recourse.

"Jesus, Mary, I Love You, Save Souls"

"LET THESE WORDS BE FOREVER ON YOUR LIPS"

On July 16, 1992, Louise Lahola received this prayer from Jesus Christ, and He instructed her to repeat it, over and over, throughout the day.

"Jesus, My Lord, I offer You all that I do, all that I say, all that I hear, all that I see; and I pray for Your unending mercy to continue to be poured upon me and my family, neighbors and friends - even those who have turned away from You and those whose hearts are like stone."

STATIONS OF THE CROSS

1st STATION

Jesus is condemned to death by Pilate. How often I judge people unjustly. Jesus forgive me for it. I see people only from the outside. You know them from the inside. Help me to leave all judgements to You. I will give them the benefit of the doubt.

LORD JESUS CRUCIFIED HAVE MERCY ON ME

2nd STATION

Jesus takes up His Cross to carry it to Calvary. You showed a ready obedience in taking up Your Cross. I often forget that it takes strength to obey, not weakness. Forgive my disobedience. Since all lawful authority comes from God, I am really obeying You out of love.

LORD JESUS CRUCIFIED HAVE MERCY ON ME

3rd STATION

Jesus falls the first time. You Fell, O Jesus, because Your human body was weak. I too am weak, so sometimes I fall. But I will always rise, and keep trying to please You, because I love You.

LORD JESUS CRUCIFIED HAVE MERCY ON ME

43

4th STATION

Jesus meets His Mother Mary. Mary's mission was to <u>give Christ to the world</u>. My mission as a Christian is to give Christ to the world. By my Christlike life I show Christ to my fellowmen. Help me to do this, O Jesus.

LORD JESUS CRUCIFIED HAVE MERCY ON ME

5th STATION

Simon of Cyrene helps Jesus carry His Cross. I am too selfish, Jesus. I love myself too much. I don't love you enough. Particularly, I don't <u>love</u> my neighbor enough, especially if I don't like him. A Cross is lighter when two carry it. Give me a great love for my neighbor, so that I will help him carry his Crosses, by my kindness, in word and action.

LORD JESUS CRUCIFIED HAVE MERCY ON ME

6th STATION

Veronica wipes the face of Jesus with her veil. Veronica had <u>courage</u>, Lord. She went fearlessly to Christ, in spite of the soldiers. I am a coward. I'm afraid to do what I should because I fear what people will think or say, ridicule, or criticize. Help me use the courage that the Holy Spirit gave my soul at Confirmation.

LORD JESUS CRUCIFIED HAVE MERCY ON ME

7th STATION

Jesus falls the second time. I often fall, Jesus, because I <u>take chances</u>. I expose myself to dangerous occasions of sin. Because sin is un-love I will not take chances on sinning, because I do want to love You.

LORD JESUS CRUCIFIED HAVE MERCY ON ME

8th STATION

The women of Jerusalem weep for Christ. How many times, Jesus, have I told You that I'm <u>sorry</u> for my sins? But how many times have I been sorry enough to change my ways? If I really love someone, I try my best not hurt them. And if I hurt them, I am deeply sorry, and firmly determined not to hurt them again. Is that the way I act to You, my God?

LORD JESUS CRUCIFIED HAVE MERCY ON ME

9th STATION

Jesus falls the third time. I get <u>discouraged</u>, Lord, when I fall again and again. But never let me lose <u>hope</u>. Never let me despair. Your strength and Your love for me can do what I cannot do alone. I will get this divine strength and love regularly through prayer and the sacraments. You said: "My grace is enough for You." I trust You, Lord.

LORD JESUS CRUCIFIED HAVE MERCY ON ME

10th STATION

Jesus is stripped of His clothes. How much do I value <u>modesty and purity</u>, Lord. My body was made by God, and it is good. He gave me the power of giving life and giving love, two most precious gifts. My body is sacred. I will reverence it. I will reverence the bodies of others. Especially, since You come into my body in Holy Communion, and God is in me!

LORD JESUS CRUCIFIED HAVE MERCY ON ME

11th STATION

Jesus is nailed to the Cross. If I had nails driven through the palms of my hands, and through my feet, I would probably faint from the <u>suffering</u>. I hate suffering. But so did You, Lord. I know, however, that I must suffer sometimes in my life. I can either waste it by resenting it, or I can accept it, out of love for You and to make up for my sins. Then it, has a saving value, as Your suffering did.

LORD JESUS CRUCIFIED HAVE MERCY ON ME

12th STATION

Jesus dies on the Cross. You died, O Jesus. <u>I will die</u> too. I don't know when. I don't know where.

46

I don't know how. My earthly life will end. My eternity will begin. You said we should always be ready. I will stay in Your love and grace always. Then I will always be ready.

   LORD JESUS CRUCIFIED HAVE MERCY ON ME

13th STATION

Jesus is taken down from the Cross. Your sacred Body is laid in the arms of Your Mother. She receives You with love and reverence. I receive Your sacred Body in the Eucharist. Help me always to receive You with love and reverence, for You are my God!

   LORD JESUS CRUCIFIED HAVE MERCY ON ME

14th STATION

Jesus is placed in the tomb. Your work is done. Your Resurrection to new life will climax it. You have redeemed the world. You have offered the greatest gift: Yourself. You have shown the greatest love. Your life brought good to all people, even into eternity. Help me to live a life of love. Love for You, my God. Love for my fellowman too. Help me to give my greatest gift, myself, to You and to them, in love. Then my work will be done. I too will have brought much good to people, even into eternity.

   LORD JESUS CRUCIFIED HAVE MERCY ON ME

TO JESUS FORSAKEN

Sweet Jesus! For how many ages hast Thou hung upon Thy Cross and still men pass Thee by and regard Thee not!

How often have I passed Thee by, heedless of Thy great sorrow, Thy many wounds, Thy infinite love!

How often have I stood before Thee, not to comfort and console Thee, but to add to Thy sorrows, to deepen Thy wounds, to spurn Thy love!

Thou has stretch forth Thy hands to raise me up and I have taken those hands and bent them back on the Cross.

Thou hast loved me with an infinite love, and I have taken advantage of that love to sin the more against Thee.

My ingratitude has pierced Thy Sacred Heart, and Thy heart responds only with an out-pouring of Thy love in Thy Precious Blood.

TO JESUS, CROSS CARRIER

O Jesus, by that Wound which Thou didst suffer on Thy shoulder from carrying Thy cross, have mercy, I entreat Thee, on those who have secret sorrows which only Thou canst know. May the memory of Thy painful Cross - bearings give them strength to carry theirs, with courage and loyalty to the end. May the thought of that secret Suffering, Thou didst endure, teach them to sanctify their hidden sorrows that they may be fruitful for Thy Glory. Amen.

PRAYER OF ST. GERTRUDE THE GREAT

Dictated by our Lord to release 1,000 Souls from Purgatory each time it is said

Our Lord told St. Gertrude the Great, that the following prayer would release 1,000 Souls from Purgatory each time it is said. The prayer was extended to included living sinners which would alleviate the indebtedness accrued to them during their lives.

"Eternal Father, I offer Thee the Most Precious Blood of Thy Divine Son, Jesus, in union with the Masses said throughout the wold today, for all the holy Souls in Purgatory, for sinners everywhere, for sinners in the Universal Church, those in my own home and within my family. Amen."

St. Gertrude the Great was born in Germany in 1263. She was a Benedictine Nun, and meditated on the Passion of Chris, which many times brought floods of tears to her eyes.

She did many penances, and Our Lady appeared to her many times. Her holy Soul passed away in 1334. November 16 is her Feast Day.

"Let the little children come to me. Do not shut them off. The reign of God belongs to such as these. Trust me when I tell you that whoever does not accept the kingdom of God as a child will not enter into it."

(Luke 18: 16-17)

THE MOTHER

The Most Important Person...on earth is a mother. She cannot claim the honor of having built Notre Dame Cathedral. She need not. She has built something more magnificent than any cathedral - a dwelling for an Immortal soul, the tiny perfection of her baby's body...The Angels have not been blessed with such a grace. They cannot share in God's Creative miracle to bring new saints to Heaven. Only a human mother can. Mothers are closer to God the Creator than any other creature. God joins forces with mothers in performing this act of creation.

What on God's good earth is more glorious than this: to be a mother.

                              Joesph Cardinal Mindszentry

PRAYER FOR DAILY NEGLECTS

Eternal Father, I offer Thee the Sacred Heart of Jesus, with all Its love, all Its sufferings and all Its Merits.

First — To expiate all the sins I have committed this day and during my life. Glory be to the Father, etc.

Second — To purify the good I have done badly this day and during all my life. Glory to be the Father, etc.

Third — To supply for the good I ought to have done, and that I have neglected this day and during all my life. Glory be to the Father, etc.

A Poor Clare Sister, who had just died, appeared to her Abbess, who was praying for her, and said to her, "I went straight to Heaven, for, by means of this prayer, recited every evening, I paid all my debts."

Life and Love Your Gift From God

PRAYER TO PROTECT LIFE

Loving God, I thank you for the gift of life you gave and continue to give me and to all of us.

Merciful God, I ask your pardon and forgiveness for my own failure and the failure of all people to respect and foster all forms of life in our universe.

Gracious God, I pray that with your grace, I and all people will reverence, protect, and promote all life and that we will be especially sensitive to the life of the unborn, the abused, neglected, disabled, and the elderly. I pray, too, that all who make decisions about life in any form will do so with wisdom, love, and courage.

Living God, I praise and glorify you as Father, Source of all life, as Son, Savior of our lives, and as Spirit, Sanctifier of our lives. Amen.

Sister Mary Margaret Johanning, S.S.N.D
Nihil Obstat: Joseph F. Martino
Imprimatur: Anthony Cardinal Bevilacqua
Archbishop of Phila., June 1994

GOD'S MESSAGE FOR LIFE

This new day is given to us, uncluttered, fresh and clean. Yesterday's troubles are in the past, tomorrow's may never be seen. God has granted us this new day to do with as we will. Let's fill it with kindness and happiness, love, joy and good will.

Be grateful for each new day. A new day that you have never lived before. Twenty-four new, fresh, unexplored hours to use usefully and joyfully. You can squander, neglect or use them. Life will be richer or poorer by the way you use today.

Our concern should be not how long we live, but how we live. God holds the length of your life, but you can have something to say about its width and depth. Expect great things from God and you will receive great things from God.

But you must have a tremendous faith, a deep faith, a faith that is so positively strong that it rises above doubt. Doubt is always getting in the way of faith. God expects us to keep moving. There's a big risk involved in taking on a new assignment or doing something new and we ordinarily are leery of risks.

Jesus tells a story that is very critical of an individual who's unwilling to take a risk with his master's money. As a result he is unable to give the man a profit from the funds that were entrusted to him. The result of that is not a happy one for the timid man.

Life is filled with risks. Our faith in God and in the people with whom we live, who really care about us, makes the risks worthwhile. A willingness to take risks is one of the conditions for living a satisfactory life.

Life involves decisions and movement and that involves risks. Because we have faith in a loving and forgiving God we move ahead, we take risks, knowing that at times we will make mistakes.

Our faith in God assures us that our mistakes can be corrected, that our sins can be forgiven. God expects us to keep moving, to take the risks involved with an active life. He will forgive our mistakes and sins. He will not forgive inaction.

When you need to talk to someone who will listen — try God.

CONSECRATION OF THE FAMILY TO THE SACRED HEARTS OF JESUS AND MARY

Most Holy hearts of Jesus and Mary, united in perfect love, as you look upon us with mercy and caring, we consecrate our hearts, our lives, our family to you.

We know the beautiful example of your home in Nazareth was meant to be a model for each of our families. We hope to have, with your help, the unity and strong enduring love you gave to one another.

May our home be filled with joy. May sincere affection, patience, tolerance and mutual respect be freely given to all. May our prayers be filled with the needs of others, not just ourselves and may we always be close to your sacraments.

Bless those who are present, as well as those who are absent, both the living and the dead; may peace be among us and when we are tested, grant us the Christian acceptance of God's will.

Keep our family close to your hearts; may your special protection be with us always.

Most Sacred Hearts of Jesus and Mary, hear our prayer.

A PRAYER TO OUR BLESSED MOTHER

Take my hand O blessed Mother.
Hold me firmly lest I fall;
I am nervous when I'm walking
And on thee I humbly call.

Guide me over every crossing,
Watch me when I'm on the stairs,
Let me know you are beside me,
Listen to my fervent prayers.

Bring me to my destination,
Safely every single day,
Help me with my undertaking,
As the hours pass away.

And when evening falls upon us,
And I fear to be alone,
Take my hand O Blessed Mother,
Once again and lead me home.

GOD SENT US A SAVIOR

If our greatest need had been information.
God would have sent us an educator.

If our greatest need had been technology,
God would have sent us a scientist.

If our greatest need had been money,
God would have sent us an economist.

If our greatest need had been pleasure,
God would have sent us an entertainer.

But our greatest need was forgiveness,
So God sent us a Savior.

PRAYER TO DEFEAT THE WORK OF SATAN

O Divine Eternal Father, in union with your Divine Son and the Holy Spirit, and through the Immaculate Heart of Mary, I beg You to Destroy the Power of your greatest enemy - the evil spirits.

Cast them into the deepest recesses of hell and chain them there forever! Take possession of your Kingdom which You have created and which is rightfully Yours.

Heavenly Father, give us the reign of the Sacred Heart of Jesus and the Immaculate Heart of Mary.

I repeat this prayer out of pure love for You with every beat of my heart and with every breath I take. Amen.

PRAYER TO ST. MICHAEL

St. Michael the Archangel, defend us in the day of Battle; be our safeguard against the wickedness and snares of the Devil. May God rebuke him, we humbly pray, and do Thou, O Prince of Heavenly Host, by the Power of God, cast into Hell, Satan and all the other evil spirits, who prowl through the world, seeking the ruin of souls. Amen

The Raccolta 447 An Indulgence of 3 years

HOLY WATER

Holy water is a means of spiritual wealth - a sacramental that remits venial sin. The Church strongly urges its use, especially when dangers threaten. The devil hates holy water because of its power over him. He cannot long abide in a place or near a person that is often sprinkled with this blessed water. St. Teresa of Avila wrote: "From long experience I have learned that there is nothing like holy water to put devils to flight and prevent them from coming back again. They also flee from the Cross, but return; so holy water must have great value." Keep your Soul beautiful pure in God's sight by making the Sign of the Cross carefully while saying, "By this holy water and by Thy Precious Blood wash away all my sins, O Lord."

ANONYMOUS

I asked God for strength,
that I might achieve…
I was made weak,
that I might learn humbly to obey.

I asked for health,
that I might do greater things…
I was given infirmity,
that I might do better things…

I asked for riches,
that I might be happy…
I was given poverty,
that I might be wise.

I asked for power,
that I might have the praise of men…
I was given weakness,
that I might feel the need of God.

I asked for all things,
that I might enjoy life…
I was given life,
that I might enjoy all things.

I got nothing that I asked for,
but everything I had hoped for.
Almost despite myself,
my unspoken prayers were answered.

I am among all men,
mostly richly blessed!

TO OUR LADY

Lovely Lady dressed in blue,
Tech me how to pray!

God was just your little boy,
Tell me what to say!

Did you lift Him up, sometimes,
Gently, on your knee?

Did you sing to Him the way
Mother does to me?
Did you hold His hand at night?

Did you ever try
Telling stories of the world?
O, and did He cry?

Do you really think He cares
If I tell Him things -
Little things that happen?

And

Do the Angels' wings
Make a noise? And can He hear
Me if I speak low?
Does He understand me now?

Tell me - for you know?
Lovely Lady dressed in blue.

Teach me how to pray!
God was just your little boy.
And you know the way.

SAFELY HOME

I am home in Heaven, dear ones;
Oh, so happy and so bright!
There is perfect joy and beauty
In this everlasting light.

All the pain and grief is over,
Every restless tossing passed;
I am now at peace forever,
Safely home in Heaven at last.

Did you wonder how I so calmly
Trod the valley of the shade?
Oh, but Jesus' love illumined
Every dark and fearful glade.

And He came himself to meet me
In that way so hard to tread;
And with Jesus' arm to lean on,
Could I have one doubt or dread?

Then you must not grieve so sorely,
For I love you dearly still;
Try to look beyond earth's shadows,
Pray to trust our Father's will.

There is work still waiting for you,
So you must not idly stand;
Do it now, while life remains
You shall rest in Jesus' land.

When that work is all completed,
He will gently call you home;
Oh, the rapture of that meeting,
Oh, the joy to see you come!

THE ROADS TO ETERNITY

Life is short and fleeting — eternity is long and endless. You live here a few years only - a hundred at most. Then you must pass through the portals of death to enter upon an existence that knows no end. There are two roads that lead to eternity.

The one is easy and delightful and full of earthly pleasures, but leads to endless misery. The other is rough and painful and full of sufferings, but ends in the bliss and glory of heaven.

Enter by the narrow gate - for wide is the gate and broad is the way that leads to destruction. You may not like it — you may rebel against it, ignore it or deny is, but the fact stands: an eternal existence has been decreed for each of us.

A PRAYER FOR PRIESTS

Keep them, I pray Thee, dearest Lord,
Keep them, for they are Thine —
Thy priests whose lives burn out before
Thy consecrated shrine

Keep them, for they are in the world.
Though from the world apart;
When earthly pleasures tempt, allure,
Shelter them in Thy heart.

Keep them, and comfort them in hours
Of loneliness and pain,
When all their life of sacrifice
For souls seems but in vain.

Keep them, and O remember, Lord,
They have no one but Thee,
Yet they have only human hearts,
With human frailty.

Keep them as spotless as the Host,
That daily they caress;
Their every thought and word and deed,
Deign, dearest Lord, to bless.

THE PRIESTHOOD IS A MASTERPIECE OF
CHRIST'S DIVINE LOVE, WISDOM AND POWER

"Jesus, Mary, I Love You, Save Souls"

65

THIS MAN

There was a Man, One sent from God,
Who came to Earth one day
To make amends for Adam's sin,
And show Mankind the way.

This Man, although from Heaven sent;
Is not but God alone;
Of virgin pure he was begot
A Man, in flesh and bone.

He is both Human and Divine.
In God He is the Son
But in majesty they're equal, for
The Father and He are the one.

He came to Earth in Human form
To open Heaven's door,
And suffered all, that we might live
In Love forevermore.

His back was torn by stinging whips;
A crown of thorns He wore;
His shoulders sagged beneath the weight
Of the heavy cross He bore.

And yet through all this agony
That ended in His death,
He uttered only words of love
Unto His dying breath.

PRAYER FOR THE RELEASE OF THE SOULS IN PURGATORY

Oh Immense Passion,
Oh Profound Wounds,

Oh Sweetness Above All Sweetness,
Oh Profusion of Blood,

Oh Most Bitter Death
Give the Souls in Purgatory,
      Especially _____

Eternal Rest.
      Amen

PRAYER FOR THE DYING

O most merciful
Jesus, Lover of
souls, I pray Thee,
by agony of Thy
Most Sacred Heart,
and by the sorrows
of Thine Immaculate
Mother, cleanse In
Thine Own Blood
the sinners of the
whole world who are
now in Their agony
and who are to die
this day. Amen

LITTLE CROSSES

Little headaches, little heartaches
Little griefs of every day
Little trials and vexations.
How they throng upon our way.

One great cross immense and heavy
So it seems to our weak will
Might be born with resignation
But these many little ones kill.

Yet all life is formed of small things.
Little leaves make up the trees.
Many tiny drops of water blending
Make the mighty seas.

Let us then not by impatience
Mar the beauty of the whole.
But for love of Jesus bear all
In the silence of our soul.

Asking him for grace sufficient
To sustain us through each loss
And to treasure each small suffering
As a splinter from His cross.

Prayer is the greatest power on Earth.

CONSECRATING THE TWO LAST HOURS OF OUR LIFE TO THE MOST HOLY VIRGIN

Prostrated at thy feet, and humiliated by my sins, but full of confidence in thee, O Mary! I beg thee to accept the petition my heart is going to make. It is for my last moments Dear Mother, I wish to request thy protection and maternal love so that in the decisive instance thou wilt do all thy love can suggest in my behalf.

To thee, O Mother of my soul, I consecrate THE LAST TWO HOURS of my life. Come to my side to receive my last breath and when death has cut the thread of my days, tell Jesus, presenting to Him my soul, "I LOVE IT." That word alone will be enough to procure for me the benediction of my God and the happiness of seeing thee for all eternity.

I put my trust in thee, my Mother and hope it will not be in vain.

O Mary! Pray for thy child and lead me to Jesus!

Amen

AND GOD SAID, "NO"

I asked God to take away my pride,
and God said "No."
He said it was not for Him to take
away, but for me to give up.

I asked God to make my handicapped child whole,
and God said, "No."
He said her spirit is whole
her body is only temporary

I asked God to grant my patience,
and God said, "No."
He said that patience is a by-product of
tribulation, it isn't granted, it's earned.

I asked God to give me Happiness,
and God said, "No."
He said He gives blessings,
Happiness is up to me.

I asked God to spare me pain,
and God said, "No."
He said, "Suffering draws you apart from
worldly cares and brings you closer to Me."

I asked God to make my spirit grow,
and God said, "No."
He said I must grow on my own,
but He will prune me to make Me fruitful.

I asked God if He loved me,
and God said, "Yes."
He gave me his only Son who died for me, and
I will be in Heaven someday because I believe.

I asked God to help me love others
as much as He loves me.
And God said,
"Ah, finally, you have the idea."

TAKE TIME

Take time to work — it is the price of success

Take time to think — it is the source of power

Take time to play — is is the secret of youth

Take time to read — it is the foundation of wisdom

Take time to laugh — it is the music of the soul

Take time to be friendly — it is the road to
happiness

Take time to dream — it is the highway to the
stars

Take time to look around — it is a shortcut to
unselfishness

Take time to pray — it is the way to Heaven

LISTEN TO ME

Just stop a while and listen to Me;
I have a question to ask of thee —
Why are you ignoring
My Mother?

I chose Her to be My very Own,
And greater perfection was never known.
Why are you ignoring
My Mother?

I was born through Her so we all would be
Spiritual members of one Family.
Why are you ignoring
My Mother?

I've sent her to you with a message Divine
Not once or twice, but many a time.
But still you're ignoring
My Mother.

Like a heath of graces Her Rosary she's given
To Her loving children as a Key to Heaven.
And still you're ignoring
My Mother!

She came with My message to LaSalette
But those requests have not been met
Why are you ignoring
My Mother?

I sent Her again to the cave at Lourdes,
But just as before you spurned Her words.
Why are you ignoring
My Mother?

To the fields of Fatima again She came
For Prayers and sacrifice in Her Son's Name.
And still you're ignoring
My Mother!

She descended again to Garabandal,
But you're not heeding her latest call.
Why are you ignoring
My Mother?

I sent Her to Earth from Heaven above,
So you would give Her your honor and love.
And still you're ignoring
My Mother!

When you ignore My Mother,
You ignore Her Son because to Me
She's the Dearest One.
Why are you ignoring
My Mother?

You'd better amend and do not tarry —
The ideal way to Jesus is Mary!
So stop ignoring
My Mother!

JESUS THE MAN

Nearly 2,000 years ago, God the Father sent His Son, Jesus, to personally re-establish the lines of communication between God and man. So Jesus came to Earth — in the form of a man. He was born in a stable, cradled in a manger, and grew up in a little country town in the home of a carpenter. He did not live in a palace, or live as a prince, or set himself up as a king or ruler. He did not surround himself with luxury or associate only with important people — with society's "upper crust." Jesus set out to go into every man's world and show each person who God is and what He is really like. He went out to where men were plowing fields or mending fish nets by the sea. He went to village wells where women went to draw water. He had dinner in ordinary peoples' houses, attended weddings, visited local places of worship, and even spent time with those regarded as outcasts. He fed the hungry, healed the sick, raised the dead. He brought help to the helpless, hope for the hopeless. This humble man stood among the common people in His homespun robe. His dusty feet shod in plain leather sandals. But His words released a powerful flow of love and brilliant light into the parched, darkened lives of the multitudes as He proclaimed:

*"If you want to know what God is like,
look at me. If you have seen Me,
you have seen the Father."*

74

Then he went to Golgotha and laid down His life on the cross to pay the penalty for sin — for all mankind. Once again man could come into the presence of God, unblemished and unafraid. Have you ever wondered why Jesus left the riches of Heaven to come to Earth to live the life of a pauper? Why would He let sinful men beat Him, humiliate Him, and hang Him on a cross to die? There is only one reason: LOVE. For God so loves the world, that He gave His only begotten Son. Jesus loved you and me so much that He was willing to leave His "world," where angels adored Him and all power and glory was His, to come to our world and die for our sins. When man could never reach up to Him, Christ came down to man. Jesus came to bring the message of love and hope to every man — the rich and poor, the educated and the unlearned, the leaders of society and the outcasts of His day. He lived and died so that every person could experience the love and forgiveness of God.

PRAYERS FOR A PEACEFUL SPIRIT

Slow me down, Lord.
Ease my pounding heart,
Quiet my racing mind,
Steady my hurried steps.

Amidst the confusion of my days
Give me the calmness of the everlasting hills
Help me to know the magical
Restoring power of sleep

Teach me the art of taking time off
Of slowing down to look at a flower,
To chat with a friend,
To read a few lines from a good book.

Remind me each day
That there is more to life
Than increasing its speed.

Let me look upwards
Into the branches of a towering oak,
And know that it grew great and strong
Because it grew slowly and well.

Slow me down, Lord.
Teach me to be gentle and humble of heart,
So that I may find rest for my soul.

PRAYER TO BE SAID BY A SICK PERSON

May be used for a novena

O Merciful Infant Jesus! I know of Your miraculous deeds for the sick. How many diseases You cured during Your blessed life on Earth, and how many venerators of Your Miraculous image ascribe to You their recovery and deliverance from most painful and hopeless maladies. I know, indeed, that a sinner like me has merited his sufferings and has no right to ask for favors. But in view of the innumerable graces and the miraculous cures granted even to the greatest sinners through the veneration of Your holy infancy, particularly in the miraculous statue of Prague or in representations of it, I exclaim with the greatest assurance: O most loving Infant Jesus, full of pity, You can cure me if You will! Do not hesitate, O Heavenly Physician, if it be Your will that I recover from this present illness; extend You most holy hands, and by Your power take away all pain and infirmity, so that my recovery may be due, not to natural remedies, but to You alone. If, however, You in Your inscrutable wisdom have determined otherwise, then at least restore my soul to perfect health, and fill me with heavenly consolation and blessing, that I may be like You, O Jesus, in my sufferings, and may glorify Your providence until, at the death of my body, You bestow on me eternal life. Amen

THE 15 PRAYERS OF SAINT BRIDGET AND THE 21 PROMISES

The fifteen prayers revealed by Our Lord to Saint Bridget of Sweden in the Church of St. Paul at Rome are published under sanction of the Decree of November 18, 1966, published in the Acta Apostolicae Sedis, Vol. 58, No. 16 of December 29, 1966.

MAGNIFICENT PROMISE TO SAINT BRIDGET OF SWEDEN

Pope Benedict XV expressed himself as follows on the Revelations of St. Bridget:

"The approbation of such revelations implies nothing more than, after mature examination, it is permissible to publish them for the unit of the faithful. Though they don't merit the same credence as the truths of religion, one can, however, believe them out of human faith, conforming to the rules of prudence by which they are probable, and supported by sufficient motives that one might believe in them piously.

The 14th of June 1303, at moment Bridget was born, Benedict, the curate of Rasbo, prayed for the happy deliverance of Ingeborde. Suddenly he found himself enveloped by a luminous cloud out of which Our Lady appeared:

"A child has been born at Birger; her voice will be heard by the entire world."
Sagii, die XXIV Aprilis 1903 Imprimatur

F.J. Girard, V.G.

These Prayers and these Promises have been copied from a book printed in Toulouse in 1740 and published by the P. Adrien Parvilliers of the Company of Jesus, Apostolic Missionary of the Holy Land, with approbation, permission and recommendation to distribute them.

Parents and teachers who will read them to young infants for at least one year will assure their being preserved for life from any grave accident which would involve the loss of one of their five senses.

Pope Pius IX took cognizance of these Prayers with the prologue; he approved them May 31, 1862, recognizing them as true and for the good of souls.

This sentence of Pope Pius IX has been confirmed by the realization of the promises by all persons who have recited the prayers and by numerous supernatural facts by which God wanted to make known their exact truth. A collection of small books, these prayers among them, was approved by the Great Congress of Malines of August 22, 1863.

Question — Must one recite the Prayers every day without interruption to obtain the privileges?

Answer — One should miss saying them as few times as possible; but if for a serious reason one is obliged to miss them, one doesn't lose the privileges attached to them, as long as one recited 5480 Prayers during the year. Once must say them with devotion and concentrate on the words one pronounces.

These prayers can serve as the Way of the Cross.

Visitors to the Church of St. Paul at Rome can see the crucifix, above the Tabernacle in the Blessed Sacrament Chapel, sculptured by Pierre Cavallini, before which St. Bridget knelt when she received these 15 Prayers from Our Lord. The following inscription is placed in the church to commemorate the event: "Pendentis, Pendente Dei verba accepit aure accipit et verbal cords Brigitta Deum. Anno Jubilei MCCCL."

As St. Bridget for a long time wanted to know the number of blows Our Lord received during His Passion, He one day appeared to her and said: "I received 5480 blows on My Body. If you wish to honor them in some way, say 15 Our Fathers and 15 Hail Marys with the following Prayers (which He taught her) for a whole year. When the year is up, you will have honored each one of My Wounds."

Our Lord made the following promised to anyone who recited the 15 St. Bridget Prayers for a whole year:

PROMISES

1. I will deliver 15 souls of his lineage from Purgatory.

2. 15 souls of his lineage will be confirmed and preserved in grace

3. 15 sinners of his lineage will be converted.

4. Whoever recited these Prayers will attain the first degree of perfection.

5. 15 days before his death I will give him My Precious Body in order that he may escape eternal starvation; I will give him My Precious Blood to drink lest he thirst eternally.

6. 15 days before his death he will feel a deep contrition for all his sins and will have a perfect knowledge of them.

7. I will place before him the sign of My Victorious Cross for his help and defense against the attacks of his enemies.

8. Before his death, I shall come with My Dearest Beloved Mother.

9. I shall graciously receive his soul, and will lead it into eternal joys.

10. And having led it there I shall give him a special draught from the fountain of My Deity, something I will not for those who have not recited My Prayers.

11. Let it be known that whoever may have been living in a state of mortal sin for 30 years, but who will recite devoutly, or have the intention

to recite these Prayers, the Lord will forgive him all his sins.

12. I shall protect him from strong temptations.

13. I shall preserve and guard his 5 senses.

14. I shall preserve him from a sudden death.

15. His soul will be delivered from eternal death.

16. He will obtain all he asks for from God and the Blessed Virgin.

17. If he has lived all his life doing his own will and he is to die the next day, his life will be prolonged.

18. Every time one recited these Prayers he gains 100 days indulgence.

19. He is assured of being joined to the supreme Choir of Angels.

20. Whoever teaches these Prayers to another, will have continuous joy and merit which will endure eternally.

21. There where these Prayers are being said or will be said in the future God is present with His grace.

PRAYERS

Each prayer is preceded by one Our Father and one Hail Mary.

Our Father, who art in heaven, hallowed be thy name, thy kingdom come, thy will be done on earth as it is in heaven. Give us this day our daily bread and forgive us our trespasses as we forgive those who trespass against us, and lead us not into temptation but deliver us from evil. For thine is the kingdom, and the power, and the glory, for ever and ever. Amen.

Hail Mary, full of grace, the Lord is with thee: blessed art thou among women, and blessed is the fruit of thy womb, Jesus. Holy Mary, Mother of God, pray for us sinners, now, and at the hour of our death. Amen.

FIRST PRAYER

Our Father – Hail Mary

O Jesus Christ! Eternal Sweetness to those who love Thee, joy surpassing all joy and all desire, Salvation and Hope of all sinners, Who hast proved that Thou hast no greater desire than to be among men, even assuming human nature at the fullness of time for the love of men, recall all the sufferings Thou hast endured from the instant of Thy conception, and especially during Thy

Passion, as it was decreed and ordained from all eternity in the Divine plan.

Remember, O Lord, that during the Last Supper with Thy disciples, having washed their feet, Thou gavest them Thy Most Precious Body and Blood, and while at the same time thou didst sweetly console them, Thou didst foretell them Thy coming Passion.

Remember the sadness and bitterness which Thou didst experience in Thy Soul as Thou Thyself bore witness saying: "My Soul is sorrowful even unto death."

Remember all the fear, anguish and pain that Thou didst suffer in Thy delicate Body before the torment of the Crucifixion, when, after having prayed three times, bathed in a sweat of blood, Thou wast betrayed by Judas, Thy disciple, arrested by the people of a nation Thou hadst chosen and elevated, accused by false witnesses, unjustly judged by three judges during the flower of Thy youth and during the solemn Paschal season.

Remember that Thou wast despoiled of Thy garments and clothed in those of derision; that Thy Face and Eyes were veiled, that Thou wast buffeted, crowned with thorns, a reed placed in Thy Hands, that Thou was crushed with blows and overwhelmed with affronts and outrages.

In memory of all these pains and sufferings which Thou didst endure before Thy Passion on the Cross, grant me before my death true contrition, a sincere and entire confession, worthy satisfaction and the remission of all my sins. Amen.

SECOND PRAYER

Our Father – Hail Mary

O Jesus! True liberty of angels, Paradise of delights, remember the horror and sadness which Thou didst endure when Thy enemies, like furious lions, surrounded Thee, and by thousands of insults, spits, blows, lacerations and other unheard-of-cruelties, tormented Thee at will. In consideration of these torments and insulting words, I beseech Thee, O my Saviour, to deliver me from all my enemies, visible and invisible, and to bring me, under Thy protection, to the perfection of eternal salvation. Amen.

THIRD PRAYER

Our Father – Hail Mary

O Jesus! Creator of Heaven and earth Whom nothing can encompass or limit, Thou Who dost enfold and hold all under Thy Loving power, remember the very bitter pain Thou didst suffer when the Jews nailed Thy Sacred Hands and Feet to the Cross by blow after blow with big blunt nails, and not finding Thee in a pitiable enough state to satisfy their rage, they enlarged Thy Wounds, and added pain to pain, and with indescribable cruelty stretched Thy Body on the Cross, pulled Thee from all sides, thus dislocating Thy Limbs.

I beg of Thee, O Jesus, by the memory of this most Loving suffering of the Cross, to grant me the grace to fear Thee and to Love Thee. Amen.

FOURTH PRAYER

Our Father – Hail Mary

O Jesus! Heavenly Physician, raised aloft on the Cross to heal our wounds with Thine, remember the bruises which Thou didst suffer and the weakness of all Thy Members which were distended to such a degree that never was there pain like unto Thine. From the crown of Thy Head to the Soles of Thy Feet there was not one spot on Thy Body that was not in torment, and yet, forgetting all Thy sufferings, Thou didst not cease to pray to Thy Heavenly Father for Thy enemies, saying: "Father forgive them for they know not what they do."

Through this great Mercy, and in memory of this suffering, grant that the remembrance of Thy Most Bitter Passion may effect in us a perfect contrition and the remission of all our sins. Amen.

FIFTH PRAYER

Our Father – Hail Mary

O Jesus! Mirror of eternal splendor, remember the sadness which Thou experienced, when contemplating in the light of Thy Divinity the predestination of those who would be saved by the merits of Thy Sacred Passion, Thou didst see at the same time, the great multitude of reprobates who would be damned for their sins, and Thou didst complain bitterly of those hopeless lost and unfortunate sinners.

Through this abyss of compassion and pity, and especially through the goodness which Thou displayed to the good thief when Thou saidst to him: "This day, thou shalt be with Me in Paradise." I beg of Thee, O Sweet Jesus, that at the hour of my death, Thou wilt show me mercy. Amen.

SIXTH PRAYER

Our Father – Hail Mary

O Jesus! Beloved and most desirable King, remember the grief Thou didst suffer, when naked and like a common criminal, Thou was fastened and raised on the Cross, when all Thy relatives and friends abandoned Thee, except Thy Beloved Mother, who remained close to Thee during Thy agony and whom Thou didst entrust to Thy faithful disciple when Thou saidst to Mary: "Woman, behold thy son!" and to St. John: "Son, behold thy Mother!"
I beg of Thee O my Saviour, by the sword of sorrow which pierced the soul of Thy holy Mother, to have compassion on me in all my affliction and

tribulations, both corporal and spiritual, and to assist me in all my trials, and especially at the hour of my death. Amen.

SEVENTH PRAYER

Our Father – Hail Mary

O Jesus! Inexhaustible Fountain of compassion, Who by a profound gesture of Love, said from the Cross: "I thirst!" suffered from the thirst for the salvation of the human race. I beg of Thee O my Saviour, to inflame in our hearts the desire to tend toward perfection in all our acts; and to extinguish in us the concupiscence of the flesh and the ardor of worldly desires. Amen.

EIGHTH PRAYER

Our Father – Hail Mary

O Jesus! Sweetness of hearts, delight of the spirit, by the bitterness of the vinegar and gall which Thou didst taste on the Cross for Love of us, grant us the grace to receive worthily Thy Precious Body and Blood during our life and at the hour of our death, that they may serve as a remedy and consolation for our souls. Amen.

NINTH PRAYER

Our Father – Hail Mary

O Jesus! Royal virtue, joy of the mind, recall the pain Thou didst endure when, plunged in an ocean of bitterness at the approach of death, insulted, outraged by the Jews, Thou didst cry out in a loud voice that Thou was abandoned by Thy Father, saying: "My God, My God, why hast Thou forsaken me?"

Through this anguish, I beg of Thee, O my Saviour, not to abandon me in the terrors and pains of my death. Amen.

TENTH PRAYER

Our Father – Hail Mary

O Jesus! Who art the beginning and end of all things, life and virtue, remembers that for our sakes Thou was plunged in an abyss of suffering from the soles of Thy Feet to the crown of Thy Head. In consideration of the enormity of Thy Wounds, teach me to keep, through pure love, Thy Commandments, whose way is wide and easy for those who love Thee. Amen.

ELEVENTH PRAYER

Our Father – Hail Mary.

O Jesus! Deep abyss of mercy, I beg of Thee, in memory of Thy Wounds which penetrated to the very marrow of Thy Bones and to the depth of Thy being, to draw me, a miserable sinner, overwhelmed by my offenses, away from sin and to hide me from Thy Face justly irritated against me, hide me in Thy wounds, until Thy anger and just indignation shall have passed away. Amen.

TWELFTH PRAYER

Our Father – Hail Mary

O Jesus! Mirror of Truth, symbol of unity, bond of charity, remember the multitude of wounds with which Thou wast afflicted from head to foot, torn and reddened by the spilling of Thy adorable Blood. O great and universal pain, which Thou didst suffer in Thy virginal flesh for love of us! Sweetest Jesus! What is there that Thou couldst have done for us which Thou has not done! May the fruit of Thy suffering be renewed in my soul by the faithful remembrance of Thy Passion, and may Thy love increase in my heart each day, until I see Thee in eternity: Thou Who art the treasure of every real good and every joy, which I beg Thee to grant me, O Sweetest Jesus, in heaven. Amen.

THIRTEENTH PRAYER

Our Father – Hail Mary

O Jesus! Strong Lion, Immortal and Invincible King, remember the pain which Thou didst endure when all Thy strength, both moral and physical, was entirely exhausted, Thou didst bow Thy Head, saying: "It is consummated!"

Through this anguish and grief, I beg of Thee Lord
Jesus, to have mercy on me at the hour of my
death when my mind will be greatly troubled and
my soul will be in anguish. Amen.

FOURTEENTH PRAYER

Our Father – Hail Mary

O Jesus! Only Son of the Father, Splendor and
Figure of His Substance, remember the simple
and humble recommendation Thou didst make of
Thy Soul to Thy Eternal Father, saying: "Father,
into Thy Hands I commend My Spirit!" And with
Thy Body all torn, and Thy Heart Broken, and the
bowels of Thy Mercy open to redeem us, Thou
didst Expire. By this Precious Death, I beg of Thee
O King of Saints, comfort me and help me to resist
the devil, the flesh and the world, so that being
dead to the world I may live for Thee alone. I beg
of Thee at the hour of my death to receive me, a
pilgrim and an exile returning to Thee. Amen.

FIFTEENTH PRAYER

Our Father – Hail Mary

O Jesus! True and fruitful Vine! Remember the
abundant outpouring of Blood which Thou didst so
generously shed from Thy Sacred Body as juice
from grapes in a wine press. From Thy Side,
pierced with a lance by a soldier, blood and water
issued forth until there was not left in Thy Body a

single drop, and finally, like a bundle of myrrh lifted to the top of the Cross Thy delicate Flesh was destroyed, the very Substance of Thy Body withered, and the Marrow of Thy Bones dried up.

Through this bitter Passion and through the outpouring of Thy Precious Blood, I beg of Thee, O Sweet Jesus, to receive my soul when I am in my death agony. Amen.

CONCLUSION

O Sweet Jesus! Pierce my heart so that my tears of penitence and love will be my bread day and night; may I be converted entirely to Thee, may my heart be Thy perpetual habitation, may my conversation be pleasing to Thee, and may the end of my life be so praiseworthy that I may merit Heaven and there with Thy saints, praise Thee forever. Amen.

A PRAYER FOR THOSE WHO LIVE ALONE

I live alone, Dear Lord.
Stay by my side.
In all my daily needs,
Be Thou my guide.

Grant me good health,
For that, indeed, I pray
To carry on my work
From day to day.

Keep pure my mind,
My thoughts, my every deed,
Let me be kind, unselfish,
In my neighbor's need.

Space me from fire, from flood
Malicious tongues,
From thieves, from fear,
And evil ones.

If sickness or an accident befall,
Then humbly, Lord, I pray,
Hear Thou my call.
And when I'm feeling low
Or in despair,
Lift up my heart
And help me in my prayer.

I live alone, Dear Lord,
Yet have no fear,
Because I feel Your presence
Ever near.
Amen

Made in the USA
Monee, IL
31 May 2021